15

Kjartan Poskitt & S

C000179620

The 99 DON'TS...

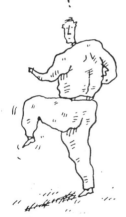

A GUIDE TO
UNRECOMMENDABLE PRACTICES

GRUB STREET · LONDON

* This edition contains 1̶0̶ extra 'Don'ts' completely FREE

AUTHOR'S NOTE:

In the best interests of our readers, the publishers
have produced this economy edition in black and white.
However, the true majesty of a more expensive
colour edition may be obtained by taking a red pen and
colouring in the airborne particles on page 75

Published by Grub Street
The Basement, 10 Chivalry Road, London SW11 1HT

Copyright © Grub Street 1992
Text Copyright © Kjartan Poskitt 1992
Drawings Copyright © Steven Appleby 1992

The right of Kjartan Poskitt and Steven Appleby to be identified
as the creators of this work has been asserted by them in
accordance with the Copyright, Designs and Patents Act 1988

A catalogue record for this title is available from the British Library

ISBN 0 948817 64 X

Printed and bound by Biddles Ltd, Guildford and King's Lynn

All rights reserved. No part of this publication may be reproduced, stored in a
retrieval system, or transmitted in any form or by any means, electronic,
mechanical, photocopying, recording or otherwise, without
the prior permission of Grub Street

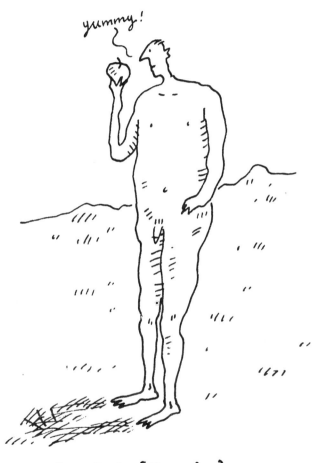

THE FIRST 'DON'T'

Don't connect up your own
gas cooker

Don't let a crab
borrow your
toothpaste

Don't bounce tortoises

Don't dress in the dark

Miaow?

and don't unravel a cat

Don't stretch your head

Don't cross your eyebrows

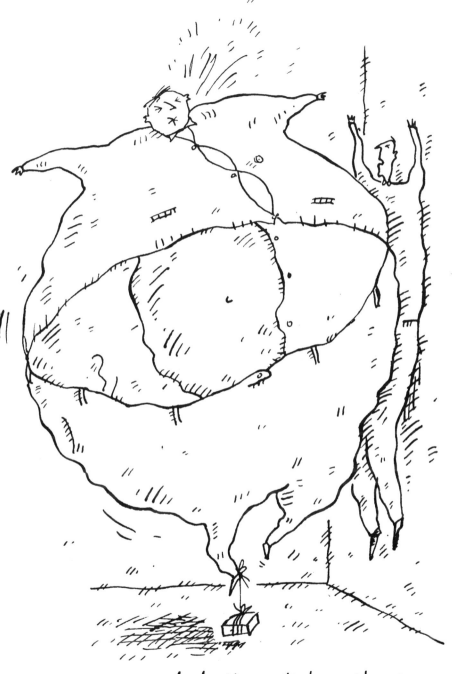

and don't just breathe in

Don't bury your house

Don't swim out too far

Don't undo your tummy button

Don't paint bubbles

Don't put your elbows
on the table

Don't watch repeats the first time

Don't splosh in puddles

Don't tattoo your head in a mirror

Don't camp in a shrink-fit tent

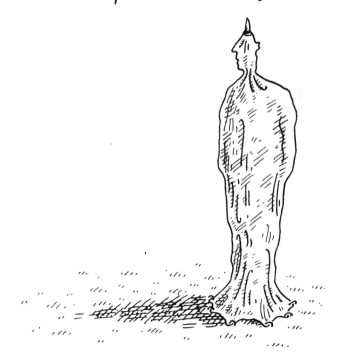

Don't reveal your true identity

SHARK LOAN COMPANY Ltd.

MADE-UP NAME _ _ _ _ _ _ _ _ _ _ _
_ _ _ _ _ _ _ _ _ _ _ _ _ _

FICTITIOUS ADDRESS _ _ _ _ _ _ _ _
_ _ _ _ _ _ _ _ _ _ _ _ _ _
_ _ _ _ _ _ _ _ _ _ _ _ _ _

RIDICULOUS OCCUPATION _ _ _ _ _ _
_ _ _ _ _ _ _ _ _ _ _ _ _ _

LAUGHABLE STATEMENT OF
INCOME _ _ _ _ _ _ _ _ _ _ _ _
_ _ _ _ _ _ _ _ _ _ _ _ _ _

DODGY REFERENCES _ _ _ _ _ _ _ _
_ _ _ _ _ _ _ _ _ _ _ _ _ _

SEX ☐   SEX ☐   SEX ☐

ILLEGIBLE
SIGNATURE _ _ _ _ _ _ _ _ _ _ _

Don't hoover your porcupine

Don't yodel anytime anywhere

Mmnnnn!!

ever

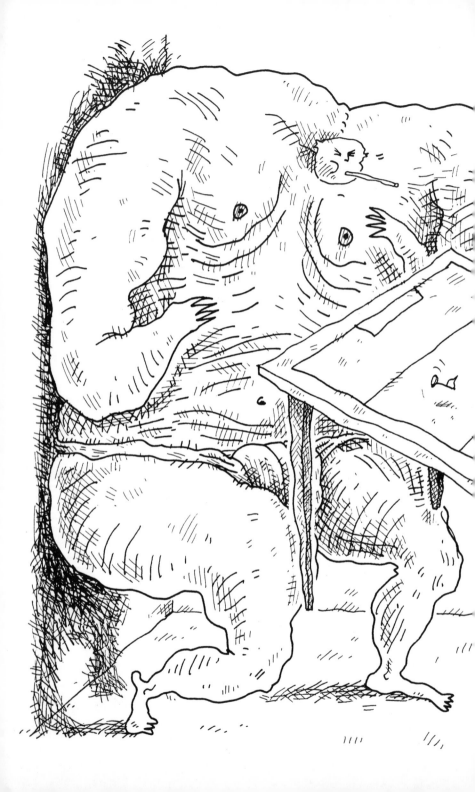

Don't challenge a sumo
wrestler to blow football

Don't turn the
light on (i)

Don't eavesdrop

Don't land on soft planets

BOING

Don't allow your socks to mingle

• 40

• 42

• 41

• 39

Don't bother

Don't buy piano six-packs

Don't fry chips in the nude

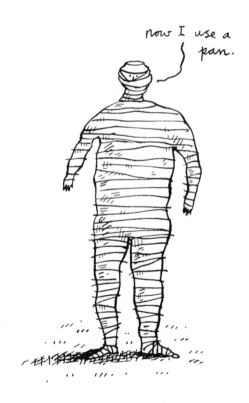

now I use a pan.

Don't assume your french is perfect

Voila!

Don't discuss Ralph Nobbs

Don't even wonder who
Ralph Nobbs is

Don't stop now!

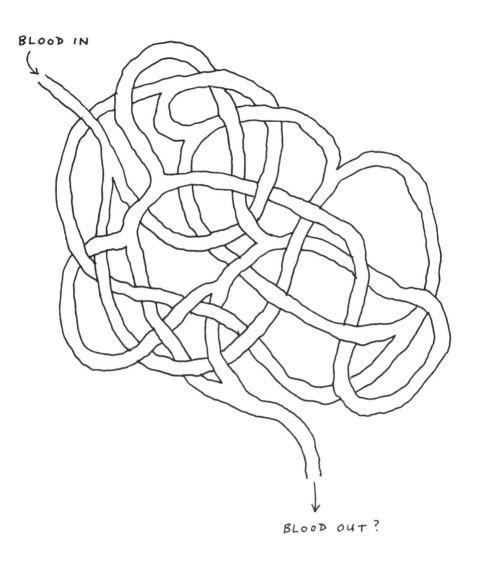

BLOOD IN

BLOOD OUT ?

Don't let an amateur
do your heart bypass

Don't order the
shepherds pie...

or the
cottage pie...

or the
ploughman's lunch

and don't steal a bus

Don't milk butterflies

They sort-of come to bits...

Don't compromise on plumbing

and don't organise spaghetti

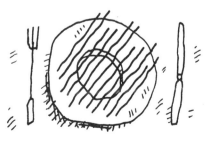

Don't say you can't deny that no-one isn't unable to be devoid of the chance to reject the incorrect lie repudiating the fact that you didn't... when you did

Don't panic in Latin

Cave! Steamrollerus venat! Proximus est!

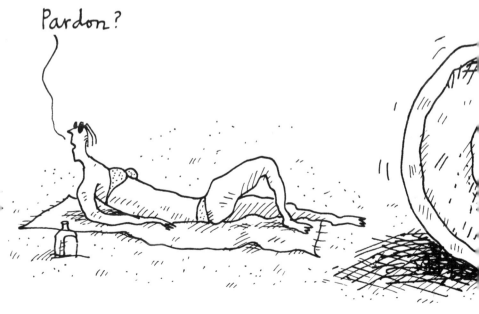

Don't eat your foot

DON'T LEND THIS BOOK!

Don't sit in big Hughie's chair

whatever you do
don't discover America

Don't assume bald people have
an unlimited sense of humour

Don't answer the door

Don't kiss too hard

Don't forget to drive on
the other side abroad

Don't believe in Popeye

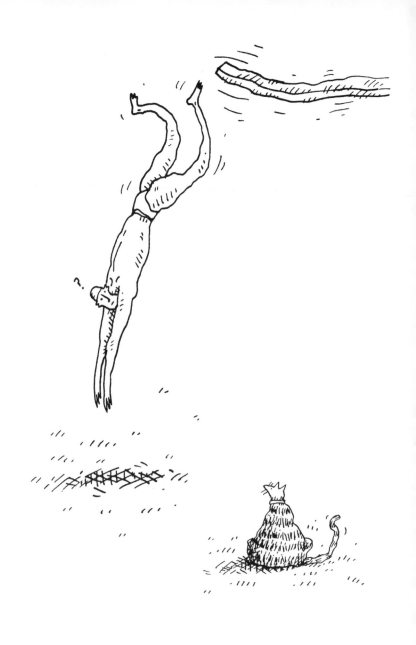

Don't move the pool

97, 98, 99...
ready or not, here
I come!

er...

Don't hide in a bottle

Don't hold onto
the shot

Don't be or
not to
be

Don't play
with your
food

cheat!

A
MOTH
TABLE

(Don't encourage moths)

Don't put your
finger here

ACME
EXPLODING INK
FINGERPRINT DETONATED

Don't pirouette in flippers

Don't trump in chess

Don't paddle in concrete

Don't practise the tuba
in a library

Don't enjoy opera

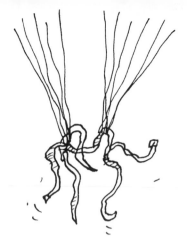

Don't adjust your braces
while parachuting

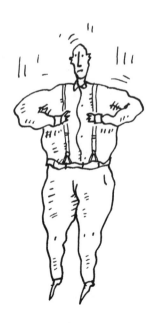

DON'T READ
ANY OF
OF THIS
TWICE

Don't dream that you're asleep because when you wake up you'll find it isn't true

Don't be <u>too</u> tall

BUMP!

Don't take
your zeppelin
to parties

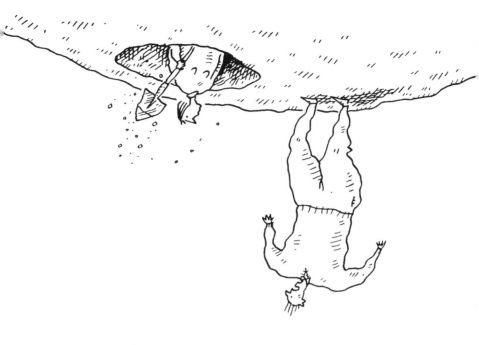

and don't dig too deep

Don't polish the runway

Don't prune your octopus

and now here is the news...

and don't experiment with your TV remote control

Don't turn the
light on (ii)

Don't take short cuts in the 100 metre sprint

Don't hire a
clairvoyant
with
amnesia

I can't
remember
the
future...

Don't build your own ringroad

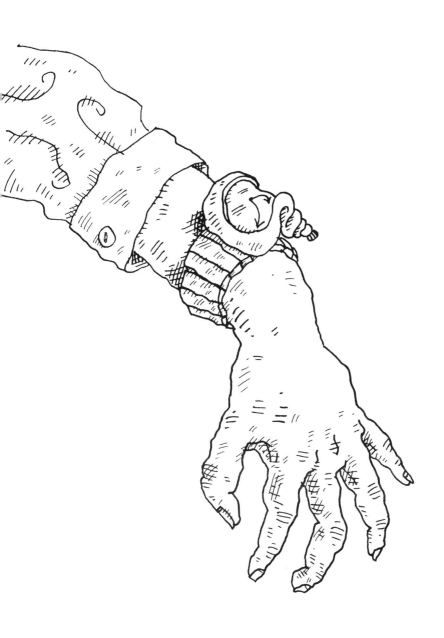

Don't overwind your watch

Don't let your
bagpipes off
the lead

Don't get distracted

Don't sneeze at the dentists

Don't keep your cactus in the sauna

Don't laugh
your head
off

At my own
joke too!

Don't hope that
mistletoe is
contractually
binding

but...

Don't pretend when it's for real

Don't let the
dinosaurs set
your unicorn
a bad example,

and don't forget
to feed your
dodo

DENNIS

Don't try to impress the surgeon

Don't write on the wrong
side of the paper

and don't wink at a cyclops

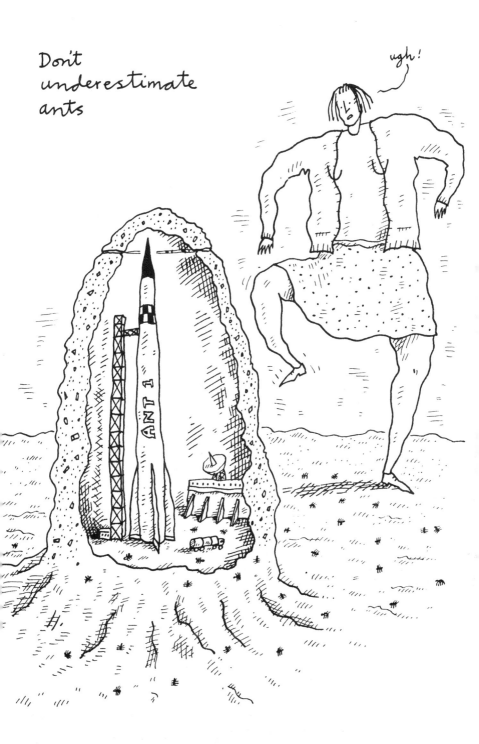

Don't turn the
light on (iii)

Don't perm your fiddle

Don't streetwalk in Venice

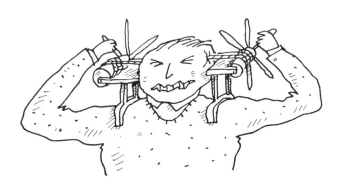

Don't rack your brains

Don't plug your satellite dish into the microwave

reception's bad...

Don't have too much plastic surgery

Don't hijack a lift

Don't... in a hammock

Don't trust gravity

Don't take earwigs literally...

super!

or pigtails...

or oxtail soup

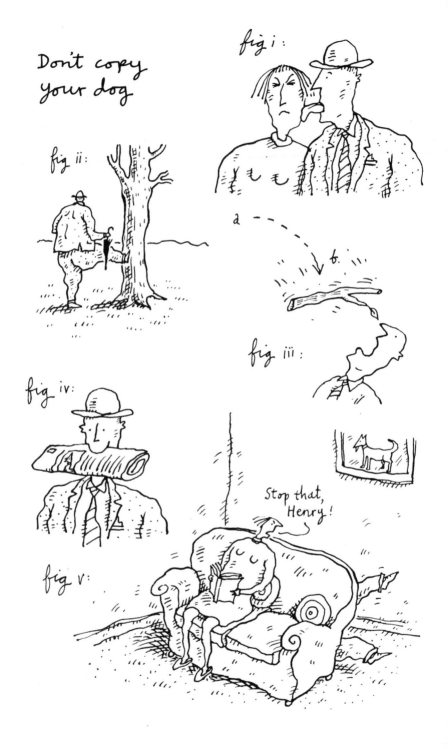

Don't do wheelies in a steamroller

Don't shuffle your toes

What ho!

Don't sublet your moustache

Don't drink draught milk

Don't drive a Ford Picasso

Don't take stairs
for granted

and finally,
don't count the don'ts!

the END

THE VERY LAST DON'T